Dominik

ZOO ANIMALS
IN THE WILD

CHIMPANZEE

JINNY JOHNSON
ILLUSTRATED BY GRAHAM ROSEWARNE

A⁺
Smart Apple Media

Published by Smart Apple Media
2140 Howard Drive West, North Mankato, MN 56003

Designed by Helen James
Illustrated by Graham Rosewarne
Edited by Mary-Jane Wilkins

Photographs by Alamy (Steve Bloom Images), Robert E. Barber, DanitaDelimont.com
(KRISTIN MOSHER), Getty Images (AFP, TORSTEN BLACKWOOD / AFP, Tim Davis,
ROB ELLIOTT / AFP, Kenneth Love / National Geographic, DESIREY MINKOH / AFP,
Michael K. Nichols / National Geographic, Manoj Shah / Stone, Mike Simons)

Printed in Thailand

Library of Congress Cataloging-in-Publication Data

Johnson, Jinny.
Chimpanzee / by Jinny Johnson.
p. cm. — (Zoo animals in the wild)
Includes bibliographical references and index.
ISBN-13: 978-1-58340-900-8
1. Chimpanzees—Juvenile literature. I. Title

QL737.P96J56 2006
599.885—dc22   2006000649

First Edition

9 8 7 6 5 4 3 2 1

Contents

Chimpanzees

Chimpanzees are noisy, lively animals. They are some of the best-loved zoo creatures. A full-grown chimp is smaller than a human. It has long arms, short legs, and a body covered with dark brown or black hair. It has no tail.

Male chimpanzees are slightly bigger and heavier than females. On the ground, chimps usually walk and run on all fours, leaning on the fleshy knuckles of their hands.

Chimps can stand and even walk upright on their back legs for short distances.

Chimpanzees are very popular with zoo visitors, and there are thousands of chimps in zoos all over the world. Older chimps may come from the wild, but most of the chimps you see were born in zoos.

Chimps move fastest and most easily on all fours.

Chimps can climb, too. Their long arms and strong muscles help them move around in trees, but they are not as speedy as monkeys.

A chimp has no hair on its face. The skin darkens as the chimp grows older.

Family life

Chimps are friendly animals and like company. They live in groups of as many as 100 but split up into smaller groups as they wander around and feed during the day.

Chimps are at home in trees and on the ground.

Zoo chimps generally live longer than chimps in the wild. Wild chimps rarely live past 50, but some zoo chimps have reached 60 or older.

Young chimps stay close to their mother. Mothers may feed and play together to help each other keep their babies safe. Males usually stay in the group they were born in, but young females usually join a new group.

Chimps like some group members better than others and have special friends.

At home in the wild

All wild chimpanzees live in Africa. Most live in rain forests, but they are also happy in woods and grasslands as long as there are lots of plants and fruit trees, as well as fresh water to drink.

There's plenty of food for chimpanzees in the rain forest.

Young chimps like to swing
from branch to branch
on their strong arms.

Chimps find much of their
food on the ground, but
they usually sleep in trees.
They will defend their area
against strangers.

If a chimp from another group comes
too near, the males hoot loudly, throw
branches and rocks, and stamp their
feet to drive the animal away.

Chimps regularly sniff
the ground and tree trunks
for signs of strangers.

At home in the zoo

Years ago, zoo chimps lived by themselves in cages, and they were very unhappy. Today, zoos keep chimps in small groups so they have company, and they give them as much space as they can.

Tropical plants help chimps feel more at home in their enclosure in the zoo.

The best zoos give chimps trees and climbing frames so they can get plenty of exercise. Keepers often give them new things to play with and hide objects and food for them to find. Chimps like to look at their visitors, but they also need a place where they can get away from people when they want to.

Play areas with ropes, swings, and trees give zoo chimps a chance to behave as they would in the wild.

A chimpanzee's day

The day starts at dawn for chimpanzees. As soon as it is light, they get up and move off in small groups to find food.

At about midday, the chimps stop for a rest. Some may curl up on the ground for a nap, while others build a tree nest, especially if it has been raining and the ground is wet. The chimps spend some of their rest time grooming one another.

Chimps spend between six and eight hours a day feeding.

During the afternoon, the chimps feed again. At dusk, the group gathers to build tree nests and settle down for the night.

A chimp makes a nest in the trees by bending branches together.

In the zoo and in the wild, chimps groom themselves and each other to remove dirt from their fur. Grooming is also a way of showing friendship.

Feeding time

Chimpanzees eat lots of different things. They like many kinds of fruits, berries, seeds, and leaves, and also eat insects, honey, and birds' eggs.

Sometimes chimps catch and kill lizards, bush pigs, and monkeys. A group of chimps may hunt together, chasing prey through the trees. The hunters usually share the meat with others in the group.

A chimp's long arms help it reach fruit at the end of tree branches.

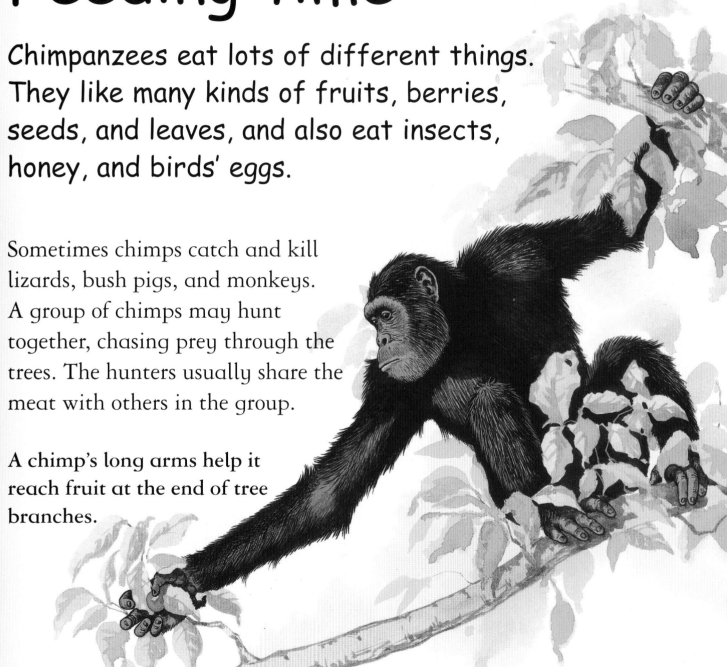

14

Zoo chimps are given food every day, and they don't have to spend hours searching for it. Keepers also hide extras, such as honey and yogurt, in the enclosure. The chimps have to search for the treats, which keeps them from getting bored.

A chimp's hands are very much like ours. They have four fingers and a shorter thumb that they can move across the hand to hold onto things.

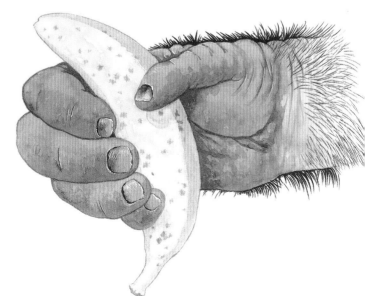

Using tools

Chimps, like humans, have learned that they can use tools to help them gather food. Very few other animals do this.

Chimps poke twigs into termite and ant nests to find insects to eat, and they've discovered how to use rocks to crack hard-shelled nuts. Chimps will also throw stones at their enemies and use sticks to help them pull down branches of fruit.

Chimps sometimes make leafy sponges. They chew some leaves until they are soft, then use them to soak up water to drink or to wipe themselves.

Chimps have learned that
when they stick a thin
twig into a termite
mound, the insects cling
to it. The chimps then pull
out the twig and suck the
insects off of it.

Keeping in touch

Chimps are not quiet creatures. When a few chimps find a tree full of delicious fruit, they make loud hooting sounds to let the others in the group know. Every chimp makes a slightly different sound, so the others know who is calling.

Chimps make at least 24 types of calls, and they have lots of different expressions, too. This chimp is begging for some special food.

A chimp's most frequent call is a "pant-hoot," with lips pushed forward.

Chimps make lots of other sounds. If a chimp is in trouble or warning off a stranger, he makes a harsh shrieking call. Little grunting noises are a sign that a chimp is enjoying his food. And young chimps laugh as they play and tickle each other.

Baby chimps

A mother chimp gives birth every five years and usually has just one baby at a time. Twins are rare.

A newborn chimp is as helpless as a human baby and spends its first months clinging to its mother's fur and traveling everywhere with her.

A baby chimp is about half the size of a human baby at birth.

The baby feeds on its mother's milk and likes to eat every hour. At night, it sleeps cuddled up with its mother in her tree nest.

The baby clings to its mother's chest or is cradled in her arms.

Zoo chimps usually start having babies younger than wild chimps. Keepers often leave the mother to look after her baby by herself, but they give her help if she needs it.

Growing up

When a baby chimp is about six months old, it starts to ride on its mother's back as she moves around. This is fun, and the young chimp can see what's going on.

This mother chimp is showing her young how to crack hard-shelled nuts with a stone.

There's a lot for a young chimp to learn—how to find food, what's good to eat, how to make nests, how to protect itself, and how to use tools.

Young chimps continue to feed on their mother's milk until they are four or five, but they start to eat other foods too when they are about two years old.

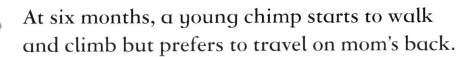

At six months, a young chimp starts to walk and climb but prefers to travel on mom's back.

Learning through play

Chimps, like most young mammals, love to play, and play helps them learn about life. Chasing each other through the trees is good practice for escaping from enemies later and helps make young chimps strong.

Young female chimps are very interested in babies and like to spend time holding and grooming them. Young males prefer to play fighting and wrestling games.

Wrestling games help chimps learn how to fight when they're grown up.

Young chimps often laugh and even tickle each other as they play.

Zoo chimps can have lots of fun on climbing frames, hammocks, ropes, and poles.

Chimps and humans

Chimps are very clever animals. They often work together as a group, they use tools, and they feel pleasure, pain, happiness, and fear just as humans do.

Chimps like to say hello or comfort each other with a touch or a hug.

A chimp's body and brain are amazingly similar to a human's. Chimpanzees have been taught to use human sign language and to use a computer to ask for treats. Chimps also recognize themselves in a mirror. Very few animals can do this.

Chimps have been trained to do simple tasks on computers.

Some zoo chimps get to know their keepers well and become very fond of them.

Chimpanzee fact file

Here is some more information about chimpanzees. Your mom or dad might like to read this, or you could read these pages together.

A chimpanzee is a mammal. It belongs to the primate family, which also includes gorillas and monkeys, and it is one of our closest relatives. The pygmy chimpanzee, or bonobo, looks very similar to the chimpanzee, but it has a slimmer body and longer legs.

Where chimpanzees live

Chimpanzees live in parts of west and central Africa, in countries including Angola, Central African Republic, Ghana, Guinea, Liberia, Mali, Nigeria, Senegal, Sierra Leone, Sudan, Tanzania, and Uganda. Most live in rain forests, but there are also chimps in savanna areas.

Chimpanzee numbers

Chimpanzees have disappeared from at least four of the African countries where they once lived, and they are becoming rare in other areas. Chimpanzees are now on the list of endangered species—they are in serious danger of becoming extinct.

Size

A chimpanzee's body measures between two and three feet (60-90 cm) long. When a chimp stands up, it is three to five and a half feet (0.9-1.7 m) tall.

Wild male chimpanzees weigh between 75 and 155 pounds (34-70 kg), and females between 57 and 110 pounds (26-50 kg). Zoo chimps are usually heavier. Bonobos, or pygmy chimpanzees, are lighter than other chimpanzees.

Find out more

To learn more about chimpanzees, check out these Web sites.

World Wildlife Fund: Chimpanzees
http://www.worldwildlife.org/apes/chimpanzee.cfm

San Diego Zoo
http://www.sandiegozoo.org/animalbytes/t-chimpanzee.html

Jane Goodall Institute
http://www.janegoodall.org/chimp_central/default.asp

Wild Chimpanzee Foundation
http://www.wildchimps.org/

Words to remember

ape

A large, tailless animal in the primate group of mammals. Chimpanzees, orangutans, and gorillas are all apes.

bush pig

A kind of wild pig that lives in forests in Africa.

enclosure

The area where an animal lives in a zoo.

grooming

Cleaning fur to remove dirt, dust, and insects.

mammal

A warm-blooded animal, usually with four legs and some hair on its body. Female mammals feed their babies with milk from their own bodies.

prey
An animal that is hunted and eaten by
another animal.

primate
A group of mammals that includes monkeys
and apes.

rain forests
Forests that grow in very hot, wet places
in tropical parts of the world.

sign language
A set of signs made with the fingers
and hands and used by deaf people.

termite
A small insect related to ants.
Large numbers of termites live
together in mound-like nests.

Index